Food around the world

Italy

Polly Goodman

WAYLAND

First published in Great Britain in 2006 by Wayland,
a division of Hachette Children's Books, an Hachette
UK Company

Hachette Children's Books
338 Euston Road, London NW1 3BH
www.hachette.co.uk

This paperback edition published in 2010 by Wayland

Reprinted in 2010 by Wayland

Editor: Sarah Gay
Senior Design Manager: Rosamund Saunders
Designer: Tim Mayer
Consultant: Susannah Blake

British Library Cataloguing in Publication Data
Goodman, Polly
   Italy. - (Food around the world)
   1.Food habits - Italy - Juvenile literature 2.Cookery,
   Italian - Juvenile literature 3.Italy - Social life and
   customs - Juvenile literature
   I.Title
   394.1'2'0945

ISBN 978-0-7502-6175-3

Cover photograph: a delicatessen in Piedmont,
northern Italy.

Photo credits: Glenn Beanland/Lonely Planet 6, Dallas
Stribley/Lonely Planet 8, John and Lisa Merrill/Danita
Delimont 9, Frank Weider/Photolibrary 10, Peter
Williams/Anthony Blake Photo Library 11, CuboImages
srl/Alamy 12, 20, 23 and 24, Rawdon Wyatt/Anthony
Blake Photo Library 13, Alan Benson/Lonely Planet 14
and 15, Robert Frerck/Getty Images 16, Rocco
Fasano/Lonely Planet 17 and title page, Norman
Hollands/Anthony Blake Photo Library 18, Juliet
Coombe/Lonely Planet 19, ACE STOCK LIMITED/Alamy
21, Donald C Landwehrle/Getty Images 22, SIME/Dutton
Colin/4corners Images 25, Karl Newedel/Getty Images
26, Stephen Saks/Lonely Planet cover.

Contents

Words in **bold** can be found in the glossary on page 28

Welcome to Italy

Italy is a long, narrow country in southern Europe. Italian cooking has been famous since **Roman times**. Italy is well known for its pizza, pasta and ice cream, which are eaten all around the world, but there are lots of other delicious Italian foods too.

▼ *Olives from Italian olive **groves** are sold in shops all over the world.*

AUSTRIA

SWITZERLAND

SLOVENIA

A L P S

LOMBARDY

Milan

Po

Venice

CROATIA

BOSNIA HERZEGOVINA

FRANCE

Parma

Genoa

Bologna

Florence

ITALY

N
W E
S

Corsica

Viterbo

Rome

Adriatic Sea

Naples

Capri

Sardinia

Mediterranean Sea

Sicily

ALGERIA   TUNISIA

▲ Italy and the Italian islands are marked in
orange on this map.

Farming and weather

Italy stretches from the Alps in the north to the Mediterranean Sea in the south. Some foods grow well in southern Italy where it is hot and dry. Other foods grow better in the north where it is cooler and wetter than the south.

▼ Farmers **harvest** their crops on the island of Sardinia.

In the north, the main crops are wheat and rice. **Dairy** cows graze in the mountains and in the **fertile** river valleys. In the south, fruits such as oranges and lemons, and many different vegetables, ripen easily in the hot sun.

▲ Grapes are grown all over Italy. They can be made into wine.

Wheat, maize and rice

Wheat and maize are Italy's most important crops. Wheat is made into different breads, such as **ciabatta**, **focaccia** and **grissini**, as well as cakes, pizza bases and pasta.

◄ Bruschetta is toasted bread with garlic, salt and pepper, olive oil and sometimes other ingredients, such as tomatoes.

Food fact

There are over 50 different shapes of pasta, such as spaghetti, macaroni, lasagne and ravioli.

Pasta is made by mixing flour, eggs and salt into a dough and cutting it into shapes. Maize is ground to make **polenta**. Rice is made into risotto, a creamy dish from northern Italy.

▲ *This chef is making sheets of pasta called lasagne.*

Fruit and vegetables

Fresh fruits and vegetables, such as tomatoes and olives, are important in Italian cooking. Tomatoes are used in salads, sauces, pizza toppings and soups. Olives are **marinated** or made into olive oil.

◀ *Insalata caprese is a salad from Capri, made with mozzarella, tomato and basil. You will find the recipe on page 26.*

Grapes are grown in every region and can be made into wine. Fresh cherries, apricots, peaches and plums are eaten after meals, or made into delicious desserts like *cassata alla siciliana* (an ice cream from Sicily).

▼ *Basil leaves are ground with a **pestle** and **mortar** to make pesto sauce.*

Food fact
Pesto is a famous sauce made from basil leaves, garlic, pine nuts and olive oil.

Meat, fish and cheese

Veal, beef and ham are the most popular types of meat in Italy. Minced beef is used in pasta sauces. Ham is either served fresh, or **cured** like salami or **prosciutto**.

◀ Carpaccio is enjoyed all over Italy. It is marinated, raw beef sliced very thinly.

Food fact
Italians use cow's milk, sheep's milk and even buffalo milk to make all kinds of cheese.

Sardines, anchovies, swordfish and shellfish are fished from the Mediterranean and Adriatic seas. Trout, carp and perch are caught in lakes and rivers. Fish is grilled, made into soup, or cooked in pasta sauces.

▲ *This man is making some Parmesan cheese by putting it into a mould.*

Shopping for food

Almost every village, town and city in Italy has a daily market selling fresh fruit, vegetables and meat from local farms. People buy the freshest food available, which changes from season to season.

▼ Oranges, lemons and nuts are for sale at an Italian fruit stall.

Most towns have a **panetteria**, which sells bread and cakes, and a general store called an *alimentari*. Some towns also have pasta shops called *pastifichio*.

▲ *This pasta shop in Naples sells every type of pasta.*

Mealtimes in Italy

Everyday Italian meals might include dishes from the menus below.

Breakfast

Crostini (little toasts)

Sweet biscuit or *brioche* (cake)

Coffee

Lunch

Antipasti including salami, stuffed peppers and artichokes

▲ *This plate of antipasti includes Parma ham, salami, artichokes, olives and sundried tomatoes.*

Lunch

Soup or pasta

Meat or fish dish
Vegetables
Salad

Fresh fruit
Cheese

Coffee espresso

Dinner

Pasta
Fresh vegetables

Coffee

▼ *Hot, roasted chestnuts from a street stall make a tasty snack.*

Around the country

Different regions and cities in Italy are known for different types of food. The northern region of Lombardy is famous for its mascarpone and gorgonzola cheeses.

▼ *Cassata is a delicious cake from Sicily.*

Many dishes are named after the places where they were first made. *Spaghetti alla Bolognese* comes from the city of Bologna. Parma ham and Parmesan cheese come from the city of Parma.

▲ *Pizza was first cooked in Naples.*

Special occasions

Italians celebrate important events with feasts. At an Italian wedding, up to fourteen different courses are served. Sugared almonds, called *confetti*, are put on the table beside each place.

◄ *Every Italian wedding has a cake covered with icing or fresh cream.*

Many towns celebrate a good **harvest** with a festival. The town of Aqualanga has a **truffle** festival, where truffles are hunted with pigs and donkeys. In Viterbo, there is a cherry festival with parades and dancing. People eat delicious cherry desserts.

▲ *In Ivrea, a yearly orange battle helps to remember an ancient fight against an evil lord.*

23

Festival food

Most Italians are Roman Catholics, and their most important festival is Holy Week, or Easter. On Good Friday people take part in street processions. On Easter Sunday, families get together for a special dinner of feast breads, Easter pies and chocolate eggs.

▼ *This Easter pie is made from over 18 layers of pastry,* **ricotta** *cheese and whole eggs.*

Forty days before Easter, people eat up the last rich foods before **Lent**. Italians celebrate by going to street parades and eating deep-fried pastries dusted with sugar. In Florence, people eat *schiacciata di carnevale*, a special carnival cake.

▼ *In the Viareggio Carnival parade, children throw sweets to the crowds from huge papier-mache puppets.*

Make Insalata Caprese!

What you need

125g mozzarella
2 large tomatoes
12 fresh basil leaves
extra virgin olive oil
salt and pepper

What to do

1. Drain the liquid from the mozzarella and slice it thinly.
2. Slice the tomatoes.
3. Arrange the mozzarella, tomato slices and basil on a serving plate.
4. Drizzle with a little olive oil, season with salt and pepper and serve.

Ask an adult to help you make this salad and always be careful with sharp knives.

A balanced diet

This food pyramid shows which foods you should eat to have a healthy, **balanced diet**.

We shouldn't eat too many fats, oils, cakes or sweets.

Milk, cheese, meat, fish, beans and eggs help to keep us strong.

We should eat plenty of vegetables and fruit to keep healthy.

Bread, cereal, rice and pasta should make up most of our diet.

Italian meals use all foods from the pyramid. They are usually quite healthy because they are mostly made up of pasta or bread with fruit and vegetables, as well as some fish, meat or cheese.

Glossary

antipasti hot and cold dishes served as a first course

balanced diet a diet that includes a mixture of different foods which supply all the things a body needs to keep healthy

ciabatta a soft bread shaped like a slipper. 'Ciabatta' is the Italian word for 'slippper'.

cured when meat is salted to make it last longer

dairy anything to do with milk

fertile land that is good for growing crops

focaccia a flat, dimpled bread sprinkled with olive oil and salt

grissini crunchy bread sticks from Piedmont

groves a small wood or planting of fruit trees

harvest to gather in a crop

Lent the period of 40 days before Easter

marinated soaked in a savoury sauce to add flavour

mortar a bowl used to pound or grind foods in, such as herbs

panetteria a bakery

pestle a club-shaped kitchen tool used for pounding or grinding foods, such as herbs

polenta a porridge made from maize cooked in salted water

prosciutto cured (salted) ham

ricotta a white cheese

Roman times the ancient Romans ruled Italy and much of Europe for over 1,000 years, from 509 BC until AD 476

truffles a type of underground mushroom

Further information

Books to read

A Flavour of Italy by Saviour Pirotta (Wayland, 2002)

Fiesta! Italy by Tereza Christie (Watts, 1997)

Kids Around the World Celebrate!: The Best Feasts and Festivals from Many Lands by Lynda Jones (John Wiley & Sons, 2000)

Let's Eat! What Children Eat Around the World by Beatrice Hollyer (Frances Lincoln, 2003)

Letters from Around the World: Italy by Fiona Tankard (Cherrytree Books, 2002)

Picture a Country: Italy by Henry Pluckrose (Watts, 2001)

A World of Recipes: Italy by Julie McCulloch (Heinemann, 2001)

Websites

CIA Factbook

www.cia.gov/cia/publications/factbook

Facts and figures about Italy and other countries

In Italy Online

www.initaly.com

General information about Italy

www.italianfoodforever.com

Lots of recipes for Italian food

Index

All the numbers in **bold** refer to photographs.